Hi. My Name is Fanny

How a stray cat became part of the family

By Darlene Maslek Colaianni

ISBN **9798696618845**

DEDICATION

I would like to dedicate this book to Tiffaney Higashi, DVM and the wonderful staff at Western Veterinary Group in Torrance California. I can not thank them enough for always taking my calls and answering my many questions. Also, for showing such compassion when we recently had to have our cat CC put to sleep.

INTRODUCTION

Hi. My name is Fanny. I was born during the spring of 2004. I want to tell you my story of how I was found and raised by a special couple and how I became friends with their other two cats.

My Story

My mom had me when she was quite young. I had three siblings and as I remember, we got along very well. My mom was great. We were her first litter. She looked after us and made sure we all ate and didn't wander off too far. I always felt safe knowing she was there to protect us. And I loved when she licked my face. That felt so good.

When we started getting older my mom encouraged us to eat out of the bowl provided by our humans and not as much of her milk. We were growing up. My siblings and I had made a game out of who could get to the bowl first or who could eat the most. And we used the litter box. Mom really didn't show us how to use the litter box but it seemed obvious that the box was there so we could cover up our poo. A natural thing for a cat to do. I was becoming a big girl and needed to act like one.

It was so much fun running around the house with my siblings. We got into some trouble like scratching the furniture or knocking something over. We wrestled and chased each other until we were so tired we fell asleep. The bigger we got the more exploring we did and the more trouble we got into. Sometimes we were put in one room to protect the rest of the home. But we always found things to do even if it meant chasing our own tails. We were always indoors although it was fun to look out the windows. We just weren't sure of what was going on out there.

Now, our humans were okay from what I can remember. My memory doesn't really start until I was about four weeks old. There was a human man and woman. They really didn't spend much time playing with us. They did make sure we had food, water and a clean litter box. They named me Smoky because of my gray color. But my siblings were called Curly, Moe and Larry after some people called "The Three Stooges" Mom was just called Kitty. I'm not sure if we ever answered to our names. We didn't care about names. But mom would get up and go to the humans when they called her. Mom always knew what to do. She was so smart and we learned from her every day.

One day, when we were a couple months old, the man placed me, Curly, Moe and Larry into a big box. He then put us in a car. It was scary because we had never been outside the house. And our mom wasn't with us. We didn't know what was happening and it was getting dark. We were crying for mom. He would drive a little, then stop. Each time he stopped he would take one of my siblings out of the box but didn't bring them back. I was the last one. He left me somewhere. I was really scared.

I was too afraid to move but when I heard noises I ran into some bushes. There were all kinds of strange noises all around. Cars, sirens, birds, people's voices. And I was getting cold.

I knew I had to do something. But what?

I looked around. Nothing looked familiar. Then I saw a man and woman walking. They walked right past me and didn't see me because I was in those bushes and it was dark. It appeared I was in some kind of apartment complex. I started crying to get their attention. They kept walking like they didn't hear me. I cried louder but they just kept walking. I started to follow them. I had to run to catch up. I was getting more scared. I couldn't cry any louder.

The man and woman started walking up stairs to where they lived. First I stayed at the bottom of the stairs then I decided to climb the stairs as fast as I could so I could go inside with them. I made it to the top of the stairs just as they closed their door.

Now what am I going to do?

I decided to keep crying. Hopefully they would open the door and help me but they didn't. I was getting hungry. How will I find food? I never had to worry about food before.

Then, I heard something. There was a man's voice coming from the bottom of the stairs. I turned around. He was calling to *me.* He was saying

"Hey, little one. Do you want a home?" Sure, I didn't know what that meant but his voice sounded friendly. I really didn't feel afraid of him. Next thing I knew I was running down the stairs and jumped into his arms. He held me and reassured me that I was safe. Maybe he knew where my mom was. Maybe he knew where Curly, Moe and Larry were.

The man took me to an apartment where there was a lady waiting for us. She called him Bill and he called her Dar. I heard them discussing how clean I was. No fleas. And they could tell I had been living with people who took care of me. Maybe they would help me get back to Mom.

I heard them opening a can. A very familiar sound. I was really hungry from all the crying I had done. I gobbled the food and wanted more, but they seemed to know I had had enough for now. I was feeling a little better. Oh, and they showed me a litter box. Right on time. *Wow, these are nice people!*

Later there was quite a surprise. I heard a growl. When I turned around there was a calico cat staring at me. Ohhhhh, that's why they had a can of cat food. And a litter box. I quickly thought she could be like my new mom so I ran towards her. Bad idea. She took a swipe at me with her big paw and I fell over. She hissed at me. Wow! That's not what I expected.

Over the next few weeks I waited for Mom. Bill and Dar couldn't find her. They made flyers and spoke to neighbors but no one said they lost a cat. No one was looking for me. So Bill and Dar became my new humans. And I became *Fanny*

As time went on, the calico, who's name was CC, started to hiss at me less. She was older than me. And she didn't like me coming into her home. I understood - *she was the boss.*

CC

AKA: The Boss

There was another cat named Mutch who I usually only saw when it was time to eat. Mutch was older too. He was shy and stayed in the bedroom closet. Didn't like to be seen. He was all white with blue eyes. I started to visit him in the closet and he seemed so nice. I think we became friends in a strange way. He was very quiet but sometimes I got him to play with me.

My friend Mutch

One day Dar put me in a carrier and took me to the Vet. I was nervous. The Vet checked me and said I was healthy. I was given some shots. There were dogs barking and the place was cold. I was glad to leave.

CC

Mutch

I always felt happy when I was with Bill. He was
the one who saved me. I liked jumping on his back
and shoulder. It was hard for Bill to walk when I
was on his back so he would call Dar to take me
off. I think he was afraid I would fall. For some
reason they laughed every time I jumped on Bill so
I tried to do it as often as I could.

My first Christmas was fun. I was about 8 months
old. There was a lot of new stuff around. A tree,

gifts, lights. I got in trouble a few times for playing and ripping some bags and paper under the tree. But on Christmas day there were gifts for CC, Mutch and me. Toys and treats. And **Catnip!** Boy was that weird.

Merry Christmas

Bill and Dar are big football fans so they liked when I played with their "Terrible Towel".

Sometimes Bill and Dar went away. I liked to hide in their suitcase because I thought that I could go with them. But while they were away a man named Chuck would come to feed us. He was Bill's brother. Mutch and I were okay but CC would act all nervous.

Please don't go.

When I was about 3 years old Mutchka died. He was 18 years old. I laid by him in the bedroom until Bill came and found him. After he was gone I really missed him. Now it was just me and CC.

CC started being nicer to me. Dar gave us catnip sometimes and we would get all crazy and play together. And CC started sleeping in the closet just like Mutch used to do. So I'd go visit her there. It was kind of like our little *hide away.*

I liked to sleep with Bill and Dar. I'd get under the covers and get all cozy. CC slept at the foot of the bed.

When I was about 9 years old Bill got very sick and went to the hospital for a month. Their niece Shellie came to help. She stayed in the spare bedroom. We didn't see Dar much since she was with Bill. I was okay, but CC was so nervous she kept pooping on the bed. I think that having someone new around and not seeing our Bill and Dar was too much for her.

When Bill came home things started getting back to normal. Shellie was gone. Bill was still trying to get better. I thought I would help him by laying in bed with him. I cuddled. I'm sure I helped him.

Helping Bill get better

When Bill recovered, he and Dar went on trips again. Chuck would come feed us. And every time, CC would get nervous and poop on the bed. Dar wasn't happy when they got home and found CC's gifts but she understood how CC was. So

Dar started putting plastic on the bed when they went on trips. It was a good idea.

The older CC got, the more she cried and begged for food and drank a lot of water. But she started getting skinny. The vet said she had kidney failure. Eventually she had to have special food.

Sometimes, in the evening, we would all lay on the bed and watch TV together. That was fun. Usually CC and I got brushed by Dar during that time. And I found out that I liked TV and sometimes would even watch it by myself if something looked interesting.

One time Dar took a photo of me as I was just finishing a yawn. She laughed and laughed. My mouth was half open and all my teeth were showing. Dar used that photo around Halloween every year. I looked really scary. Actually, I wasn't too proud of the look.

Happy Halloween

I am taken to the Vet every year for a check up. I have even had my teeth cleaned. They put me to sleep for that. When I woke up I wouldn't know where I was. I would hear those dogs barking and then I knew where I was. When I got home I was still feeling funny. I would try to walk but kept bumping into things. Dar and Bill laughed at me.

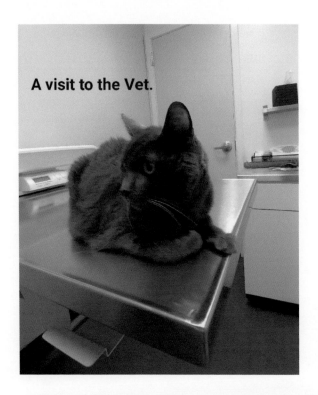

A visit to the Vet.

CC and I were getting along. I would try to get her to play. I'd bug her until she would smack me. It didn't hurt, but I would fall over so she would think she won.

Staying nice and cozy

Sometimes we slept together on the bed. CC was doing good on her special food but still skinny. I started to just lay quietly near her. Even though we didn't play as much, we seemed to be closer. I felt sorry for her. She always wanted food. And she hardly slept. She roamed around all night and howled a lot.

Naptime for CC and Fanny

Bill was retired but Dar still got up at 5:30 am to get ready for work. CC got into the habit of being fed when Dar got up so even on Dar's days off CC woke us all up at 5:30. Of course I was right there pretending to be hungry too. CC had this weird thing where she begged for food at the same times every day. 5:30 am, 11:00 am, 1:00 pm, 5:30 pm, 7:00 pm, and 10:00 pm. It was so funny how she knew what time it was. Dar made sure I got less food than CC because I would have been very fat if I ate that much.

One time when Dar came home from having surgery I made sure I kept her company. We took naps together and I kissed her a lot to make her feel better. But I also made time for Bill. I know he always needs me to show him love. It's *our thing.*

As you can see, I can always find a reason to nap.

Helping Dar recover

CC and I had a basket with lots of toys. It's funny but there were two Identical stuffed mice that we both loved. We always pulled those mice out, threw them around and made funny noises. Bill would pick them up every morning and put them back in the basket. I loved getting one out when Bill and Dar were gone. When no one was around I would throw that mouse all over the place. It was so much fun.

Who wore it better?

One time Dar made bows and put them on me and CC. She took photos of us. You know, I think I looked so much cuter in mine. You have to rock the attitude.

As time went on, CC got weaker. I didn't try to play with her anymore. And she started getting very close to Dar. Dar made sure CC had everything she needed. They were inseparable.

CC is getting weaker

My friend was taken to the Vet a few more times and finally there was a time when she didn't come home. That was in July of 2020. She was 20 years old. I was confused. I would forget and start looking for her. But she wasn't there.

I just laid around. I missed her so much. I didn't feel like eating. Then I remembered. I had never really had to ask for food before. CC was in charge of food. Dar and Bill made sure I had food and water, but I was throwing up and getting dehydrated. I was taken to the Vet and given fluids under the skin. I felt so much better but the doctor told Dee and Bill that I had Stage 2 kidney disease. So now I am eating the same special food CC was eating.

I really can't get back to normal yet. I'm still sad. Bill encourages me to spend more time with Dar. Dar cried a lot at first and we knew she was missing CC. CC left a hole in all our hearts.

And now I guess it's my time to sleep in the closet just like Mutch and CC did.

CONCLUSION

I am so lucky to be living with this lovely couple for the last 16 years. And I was blessed having time with Mutch and CC.

I may be alone now, but I know that Bill and Dar love me and will always take in any cat that needs a home. That's what they did for Mutch and CC. And then me. So maybe someday I will get another friend. You never know.

And now I guess it's *my* time to sleep in the closet just like Mutch and CC did. And wait for a friend to come visit me.

Remember: Grieving is an emotional reaction to losing a loved one. Our pets can grieve just like humans.

The mouse misses you, CC.

And so do I.

Love,

Fanny

ABOUT THE AUTHOR

I am a retired nurse who has always wanted to write but never had time. Now I am finally dipping my toe into the writing pool.

I grew up on a farm in Western Pennsylvania near the small steel town of Aliquippa. I had to find ways of amusing myself as a child since there were no kids around. That's where my love of cats came to be. We kept most of the litters and I gave all of them names. They were all outdoor cats and they loved living in the barn and catching the mice.

I used to dress a few up in baby clothes and put them in my baby buggy. One year I built a cat apartment building (we didn't call them condos back then) out of cardboard boxes. Our oldest cat, Henrietta, always came to our door when she was ready to have kittens and we would prepare her a birthing box. She would jump right in and start giving birth. And a cat named Bobby would jump on my back when I went sled riding. He started jumping on the sled and making me pull him back up the hill. Proving-cats are quite smart.

My husband had never been around cats before. In fact, he said he didn't like them. But when our first stray showed up 30+ years ago (left in a paper bag), he was smitten. So we have adopted 4 strays so far. Fanny is by herself now, so if there is a stray out there looking for a home, just come find us.

Printed in Great Britain
by Amazon